MELODIOUS DOUBLE-STOPS

(Mélodies en Doubles-Cordes)

FOR VIOLIN

by JOSEPHINE TROTT

COMPLETE
Books I and II

ED 4369

ISBN 978-1-4234-2709-4

G. SCHIRMER, *Inc.*

DISTRIBUTED BY

HAL•LEONARD®
CORPORATION
7777 W. BLUEMOUND RD. P.O. BOX 13819 MILWAUKEE, WI 53213

Copyright © 2007 by G. Schirmer, Inc. (ASCAP) New York, NY
International Copyright Secured. All Rights Reserved.
Warning: Unauthorized reproduction of this publication is
prohibited by Federal law and subject to criminal prosecution.

Melodious Double-Stops
BOOK ONE

Josephine Trott

In the first eight exercises one of the two notes is invariably an open string.
Do not lift fingers until necessary.

Copyright © 1925 by G. Schirmer, Inc. (ASCAP), New York, NY
International Copyright Secured. All Rights Reserved.
**Warning: Unauthorized reproduction of this publication is
prohibited by Federal law and subject to criminal prosecution.**

3

Moderato

4

Allegretto

5

Lamentoso

6

Scherzando

10

Vigoroso

11

Commodo

12

rit. - - - -

13 Moderato con moto

14 Andante

Allegretto

15

Andante

18

mf

dim. - - - p

Leggero

19

spiccato

20 Moderato

21 Lento

22 Allegretto

Adagio

23

Allegro

24

Tempo di Marcia

25

a tempo

p

rit.

Animato

26

mf wrist
poignet

rit.

f

2

p

2

2

rit.

a tempo

harm.
sons harm. *mf*

rit.

18

Vigoroso

27

Con grazia

28

mf

a tempo

rit.

rit.

* + = left hand pizzicato.
   la main gauche pizz.

29 Andante

30 Allegro risoluto

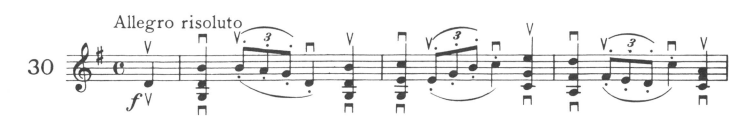

MELODIOUS DOUBLE-STOPS

(Mélodies en Doubles-Cordes)

FOR VIOLIN

Book II

to Louis Persinger, in friendship and admiration

Melodious Double-Stops
BOOK TWO
(First Position)

Josephine Trott

✳ + Pizzicato with the left hand.

Copyright © 1931 by G. Schirmer, Inc. (ASCAP), New York, NY
International Copyright Secured. All Rights Reserved.
Warning: Unauthorized reproduction of this publication is
prohibited by Federal law and subject to criminal prosecution.

2 Adagio

rit. poco a poco

3 Allegretto

rit. - - -

a tempo

harmonics

6 Leggero

7 Alla marcia

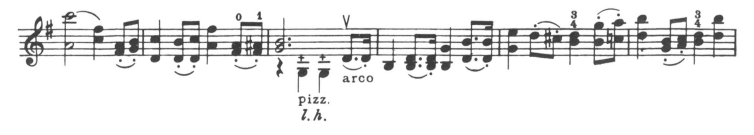

Allegretto

9

Molto marcato

10

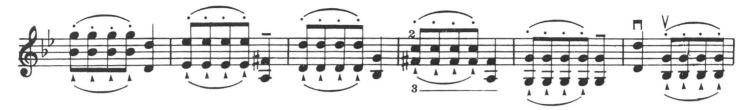

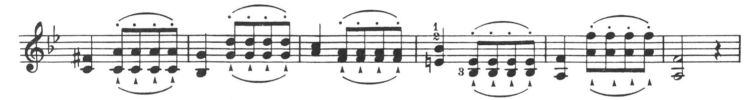

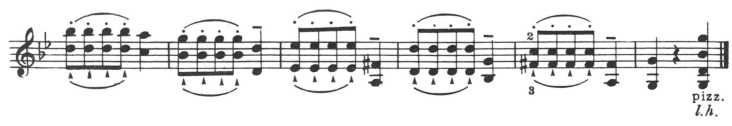

11 Allegretto

pizz.
l. h.

12 Andante

a tempo

rit.

Vigoroso
(+ = pizz l.h.)

13

Espressivo

14

stay in 1st Pos.

a tempo

rit. - - - -   *p*

Andante con moto

15

broad

harm.

Lamentoso

18

stay in 1st Pos.

Commodo

19

harm.　　　harm.　　　harm.

Leggero

20

(lift bow with wrist)

Moderato

21

Valzer lento

22

Lamentoso

23

Ben marcato

24

a tempo

rit.

Marziale

25

mf

ff

pp

rit. - - - - a tempo

26

Moderato

stay in
1st Pos.

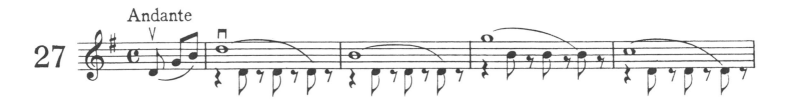

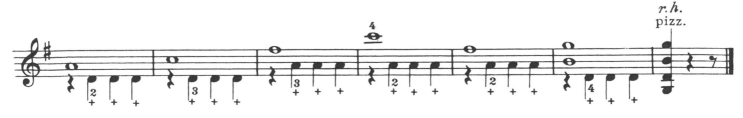

28

ricochet